# Life

## through the Eyes of a
## Fourteen Year Old

Poems

Royal Chukwudumebi

iUniverse Inc
Bloomington

Life through the Eyes of a Fourteen-Year-Old
Poems

The views expressed in this work are solely those of the author and do not necessarily reflect the views
of the publisher, and the publisher hereby disclaims any responsibility for them.

iUniverse books may be ordered through booksellers or by contacting:

iUniverse
1663 Liberty Drive
Bloomington, IN 47403
www.iuniverse.com
1-800-Authors (1-800-288-4677)

Because of the dynamic nature of the Internet, any web addresses or links contained in this book may
have changed since publication and may no longer be valid.

Any people depicted in stock imagery provided by Thinkstock are models,
and such images are being used for illustrative purposes only.

Certain stock imagery © Thinkstock.

ISBN: 978-1-4620-0900-8 (sc)
ISBN: 978-1-4620-0901-5 (dj)
ISBN: 978-1-4620-0902-2 (ebk)

Printed in the United States of America

iUniverse rev. date: 4/11/2011

To my father in heaven—
I couldn't have done this without you, Dad.

# Love

A burden always wanted
But never carried;
A spirit always hunted
But quickly buried.

A spark finally started,
Swiftly burned out.
An ocean forever parted;
A mirage cast in doubt.

A word unwisely said
But forever spoken;
A word already dead,
An everlasting token.

# Wealthier Than One

A beggar taking care of family and home;
A rich man, with everything but still alone.
The world weighs both with judgment and care,
But who in the end is found wealthier than one?

Poorer the beggar helps brother and sister;
The rich man's too busy to help a mister.
The world weighs both with judgment and care,
But who in the end is found wealthier than one?

Through the years they both become ill
While only one can pay a prince's bill.
The world weighs both with judgment and care,
But who in the end is found wealthier than one?

The dead beggar has soon left a legacy
While the rich man only left a fallacy.
The world weighs both with judgment and care,
But who in the end is found wealthier than one?

# The Scum and the gem

Of these few chosen, all bear Lies's fruit,
A word softly spoken but rarely meant
A lie tightly clung to but often said.
The scum quickly rotted and grudgingly lent
A child finally asleep and put to bed.

And these are Love's most sought-after clues.
The word rarely spoken but always meant
The truth quickly let go of and scarcely said.
A gem slowly discovered and swiftly lent
The child forever awake and never put to bed.

But in this day, which are of a nature true?
Love is softly spoken but rarely meant
A lie tightly clung to but often said.
The gem slowly discovered but grudgingly lent
A child forever awake and never put to bed.

# The Fullest of Life

Two friends by the roadside decide to part ways;
Both split their daily fares and counted the days.

Swiftly the first arrives without worries or fears;
But the second sojourns with troubles and tears.

In his paradise, the first looks for his belongings
For at the start is where they lay there forgotten.

In his journey to get back what he had left
He is taken to the edge of Death's cleft.

The second, at last, finds that his journey is ended
His mission accomplished and he restfully mended.

One lived effortlessly, and one lived in strife
But only one truly made the most of life.

# The Eternal Sage

Wisdom slowly walks;
Wisdom slowly talks,
Measures each word,
Always softly heard.

Rarely ever seen,
This eternal being;
Never being found,
But is forever around.

Teaching the unknown,
Never judges age,
More seeds sown
By this sage.

# Humanity

We are scattered around
A people earthbound.

We supply our needs
With bad or good deeds.

We are a great race
That is lost in a maze.

We edit history
And call it humanity.

But is that it?
Is that what we call this?

A race that kills
Our need is filled?

A race that lies
Calling it "great sacrifice"?

A race with no mercy
And with no courtesy.

A race with prejudice
And with no true justice.

A race that steals
To get the next meal.

A race that lusts
To have their "musts."

A race that tricks
Who's perverted and sick.

A race so proud
Giving the weak to drought.

For those not knowing how to cope
There is still a last ray of hope.

# Chances and Choices

We look for symbols and wonders;
We search for people and things.
We never sit down to ponder
But hunt for the next fling.
Do we think of our choices
Or do we just take chances?
We are a body of voices
Forever taking our last dance.
Do you think of your options?
Or are you just stuck in a trance?

# The Final Road

We walk on this lonely road,
Looking for a final abode,
Accompanied by lost strangers
Giving trust on a simple wager.

Each stride and step counted
With everything amounted.
Finding our lost dreams again
On those shard-filled lanes.

Gaining their wondrous mate,
Finally reaching that gate
Journey's end and journey's meet
Peacefully resting wearied feet.

# Loves Petition

Whispers of sweet sound
A couple together forever bound;
"I love you's" eternally around.

Is it in their eyes?
Is it in their good-byes?
Or how they never lie?

No, it's not the words
Or the person said toward
Or the two hearts that soar.

But it's why it's said.
Whether anyone frets
Make sure the love is never dead.

# The Secret Diaries of Teenagers

Secrets are whispered
And lies told.
Friends are dispersed;
The truth unfolds.

Hidden lines crossed
And voices unheard.
Lives are tossed,
Illnesses left uncured.

The death arises;
No one listens
To avert this crisis
Leaving roads crimson!

Guns are fired;
Children are dead.
Tired policemen are
Going to bed.

Their lives slowly die;
Parents just ignore.
Their teens silently cry,
Hidden within their core.

# Most Popular

The rain steadily poured down;
His friends soon left and scattered away.
He was alone without a sound;
He stood surrounded the very next day.
"Most Popular" is an outcast
Who laughs with his so-called friends,
But the facade never lasts.
He wishes it all would fade to an end
And time could then rewind.
Don't judge, for you have wanted that bind.

# The Beauty of the Storm

The wind orchestrates the songs of sounds;
Dancers of green jolt musically bound.
Chimes of glass resonate, loud and clamorous,
And the animals scatter at the loud chorus.

Hours pass; the dancers take their earned due.
Mauve curtains close its crescendo on cue.
The wind's baton finishes its last stanza,
And the animals return to their bonanza.

# Opportunity

She said, "He was dearly loved."
They said, "How have they been?"
Those words took off and roved,
Never knowing the things unseen.

No one knew how he died.
She waited, looking for him;
She found out, and she cried.
Slowly, her life turned to steam.

Who did she want to come?
Opportunity was his secret name,
And Chance was in the dome.
Now, let the hidden games begin!

# Fate and Duty

Two friends frolic together as a pair
But soon learn that they shouldn't share.
Both learned they were to forever fight
Because one was dark and the other light.

Stubbornly, they refused to separate,
And they were forged to their chosen fate.
Regarded as outcasts of their community,
But they looked on it as a duty.

In the present, they are everywhere;
"Together forever," and they don't care.
They are accepted and considered equal;
But I hope there isn't another sequel.

# The False Smile

She starts to weep;
She's been moving slow.
Having never-ending sleep,
Taking blow after blow,
Waking up with a false smile,
She sinks deeper at every mile.

Everything passes by;
Bitterness is her right.
Her innocence was taken;
She was left forsaken.
She is *Daddy's little girl*;
Her world becomes a whirl.

Stumbling down streets,
Moving to the next beat,
Mom's not picking calls up;
She takes one more cup.
Red and blue flashing lights
Make lost all she had in sight.

Walls come crumbling down;
You want out of this town.
You've already lost it all;
Just breathe and stand tall.
Open up your guarded safe;
Do the good things you've wanted,
Because your life is no more daunted.

# Inner Beauty

She eats, never missing a beat
And lives in fear of breaking her seat;
She looks in the mirror and prays,
Hoping God will answer one day.

She cries away her days,
Hearing the rumors her classmates say;
She misses breakfast, lunch, and dinner,
Trying to make herself thinner.

Further on, she gets trimmer
As this sick little game's *winner*;
Thinking beauty to the death was duty
And never seeing her inner beauty.

# Patience of the Earth

A meandering stream soundly asleep,
Lying where no man has dared tread.
Blades of luscious green so deep,
Awake from their dark, moist beds.

The brown beast lumbering by home;
The tiny creature traveling on its way.
Birds waiting for summer to come;
The lion starts stalking its vital prey.

None were told nor were they taught,
But each learned, practiced, and then did.
Quietly waiting and fighting,
Giving what they had patiently bid.

# The Prodigal Son

He walked those lonely streets of London;
Everything from his past abandoned,
Asking of others for his needs and wants,
A truthful man lost in a sea of liars.

At night his little girl cried herself to sleep;
His family wonders and weeps.
Cowardly hiding himself from their sight,
He looks and searches his lost mirage.

Three summers pass before he dares return,
Watching their eyes for hidden scorn;
He realizes all they had needed was him;
The prodigal son finally returns home.

# The Builder

Red brick and mortar,
No time is squandered.
The sun turns to light;
The creation comes to sight.
The builder had disappeared
After the roof was tiered
And the foundation laid.
With the workers paid
The builder's last words:
"It is good."

# The Breaking News

We need to finally work together,
Work past ourselves and our differences;
But what if we decide to never
Get over our preferences?

All over the news, tragedies occur;
Killing, raping, and abductions are not few.
Too consumed with things to procure,
We ignore the real and true.

If we released all of it away
And actually cared for and about someone,
Would we win and stand tall
Or not care until life is done?

# Second Looks

We laugh and take jabs,
Never taking second looks
About who we shook
Or where we stabbed.
Listen before you speak;
Watch before you pass.
One word you leaked
Might be his last.

# The Pretender and the Love

He was there when you had your first walk,
Protecting you from every stare and jeer.
He was there for every father-daughter talk
And one day, he decided to up and disappear.

He was the man of the family, always there to
Provide for his sick mom, an angel from above;
He prayed that her imminent death wasn't true.
Even after the last breath, he looks on with love.

# One Last Hit Is All It Takes

She takes hit after hit from him,
Never complaining but claiming true love,
Explaining away every bruise and broken limb.
Does he feel strong after every shove?

Day by day, she is withering away;
The beatings got worse and steadily increased
Until she finally gave up life and died one day.
He didn't care that she was deceased.

# The Eternal Battle

Time's tempo continues, never missing a beat,
But the morality is dropping on the street.
The rose of life is wilting away;
More souls dying soundlessly every day.

Kindness, goodness, charity left forgotten
Hearts are now evilly sodden.
Tiny Rays of Light gleam
Making Hearts of Hope team.

Will we seek those shimmering Rays
Fervently and forever every single day
Those with hearts that are hoping
Or stay in Darkness fearfully groping?

# Little Miss Anybody

No one hears her muffled cries,
And little by little, her spirit dies.
Little by little, she withers away;
She cries herself to sleep every day.

She walks through your school's doors
And nobody knows what she stores.
For that very day lies the death
When she'll take her last breath.

She takes one to her head;
Next day, they found her dead.
People never know how it arises;
If they knew they'd be surprised.

Miss Outcast or Miss Queen Bee,
If you looked, you would see
A hurting person deep down inside
And stopped her before she died.

# K-I-N-D-N-E-S-S

K-I-N-D-N-E-S-S
If we practiced it, we wouldn't have so much stress;
One eight-lettered word that make so much sense.
Yet we always take it in the wrong tense.

It's not in the opening of a single door,
But the emotion into it that is poured.
It's not the returning of another's money,
But the emotion afterward that tastes like honey.

Some do it for the reward—others for nothing.
If we meant it, we wouldn't want anything.
Treating others like you would want to be
Should be one thing in life that is free.

# The Hidden Attack

New devices and inventions divide us from one another
Even so much that now we don't even bother.
The blind leading the blind, and the deaf the deaf
So much that now we can see this horrendous theft.

Children, wives, and husbands all left alone,
And we think each other's beautiful voices drone.
We bypass one another, looking at familiar strangers,
Never realizing that we have present danger.

Words spurted out of hate and anger can't be taken back;
Apologies can't retract what your words lacked.
They were a direct attack upon a loved one's heart;
Now, they have torn a close-knit family apart.

# The Blind Judging the Jaded

Shopping bags in her hand
Needless thoughts in her head
Listening to her favorite bands
Next morning, she's pronounced dead.

Hands in his front pockets
Staring at fleeting passersby
With his mother in his locket
His macho façade only a discrepant lie.

Society judges them, never listening,
Sometimes just but always blind;
Leaving them drowning and sinking
In their self-created binds.

# Not Knowing How Wrong They Are

His throbbing heart encased in ice
We make him pay the ultimate price.
Some think that he cannot love
Not knowing how wrong they are.

Step by tragic step he takes;
People clear away for their sake.
Cold glances are thrown his way
Not knowing how wrong they are.

A monster they themselves have created
His heart becoming colder and saturated.
Walking alone, he can only look above
Not knowing how wrong they are.

Judges, whom themselves are unclean
Judging his innocence as they deem.
They cast and throw him away
Not knowing how wrong they are.

# A True Winner

Lies being spoken into willing ears
Are exchanged with truthful, evil lips
Bringing subjects of scrutiny to tears
And their reputation to the whips.

Beaten, broken, and left with nothing
Building those torn scraps into something
And coming out as the top winner
Invite their spiteful enemies to dinner.

# The Internal Battle

Music to my ears
That calms all my fears
How you let your emotions out
Without giving way to screams and shouts.

What would you yourself do?
When you have to measure each word, phrase, and sentence on cue
In every second, minute, and hour of every single day?

Feeling torn inside
Wouldn't you at all cry?
Being taken wrongly for your stares
Would you do right knowing the weight that you bear

But I'll try to win
Doing it for you and kin.
So bring on this long-awaited fight
And let us fight till the first sign of light.

# The Word Unsaid

Misunderstood and ignored
Left alone and bored
They're new breeding grounds.
Moving to the new sound
They're lost forevermore
Now rotten to the core.
One little word or look
Could change the road they took.
What if you …?
What you could do …?
Are questions of the past
Change your future at last.

# Unconformity

They have made their own sayings
And so approve their own slayings.
Are we really going to conform
Or do you want to make a storm?

We have been so very complacent;
Don't be blinded by their estrangement.
Get up and fight with your words
With those unbreachable swords.

You have to stop being compliant
Stop going into your murmured rants
And go to those unreachable places
Reaching those deprived faces.

# The Misguided Label

The outcasts and rejects
The jocks and prefects
Who are they to us
That make all of this fuss?
Yes, four hard years
That we all have to bear
And this is how we deal
By giving each their own seal.
Some of us are truly surprising
For in life, we start rising.
The jock that actually made it in life
The outcast that's dealt well with strife.
The reject that is now well known
The prefect, reaping abundantly what he's sown.
Before you slap on the label
First know they're capable.

# The First Place Loser

Some people give their all
Some people just quit
When not first called
And they don't get it.
There's always a last place
For those who didn't care
Those who didn't race
Those who didn't rear.
I am not one of those
But what about you?
Did you care to lose?
Did you at least try to?
Every last is a first
So lift off that curse.

# One Minute Flat

The *big day* and *final day*.
Most people wonder away
At what will all finally happen,
All of their ideas so misshapen.
Even children know when to stop
And let the theories all drop.
What does it matter if you die
By fire, ice, or a tide so high?
What really matters is now.
When Truth makes its final bow
And the end curtains close,
When Time gives its final dose,
No one can change the fact
Even in one minute flat.

# The Comforter

Tears fall down one by one,
Not stopping till they're done;.
When everything is a blur,
What can we concur?

Comfort shall and will come;
Be not afraid of this humdrum.
When they are least suspecting
Is when he'll come collecting.

# An Honorable Service

We see all of this beauty around us,
But all we do is mar its crust.
We should be its stewards,
Treating it well without rewards;
Waste not, want not.
Never letting it go to rot
Should be an honorable service,
Not hiding our wastes in its crevice.

# The Void

Hidden inside of us is a gaping hole
That is ours to fill and make whole.
Two alternatives and two choices:
Choose to listen to the voices
Or to ignore and move on.
Yours is the pro and con.
Whether you've chosen rightly
Will not be weighed lightly;
Light will indeed illuminate
And Darkness consummate.

# The Cream of the Crop

Friends from different continents
With personalities prominent
From some, lessons are learned
From others, scrapbooks burned
Molding and adjusting attitudes
From selfishness to gratitude
They are whoever they are
Even with their hidden scars.
Keep the good ones close
But the cream of the crop the most.
Never knowing who you may need
You'll have one plant the important seed.

# The Source

Secular equals popular;
Mainstream is spectacular.
Is this how you expect us to live?
By how Main Stream tells us to dress, think, and act?
If we really did this, would we really be rich and famous?
Flashing lights, clicks and clacks of our high-fashion shoes
With all of the wrong images pressed on us, doesn't it sound wrong?
Shielding us and protecting us can only do so much.
What about getting to the source?
You can't keep complaining of the *bad influence* of television. Why not change it?
The *will of the people*—are you not them?—*is America.*
Take this country—no, *your* country—back!

# Dear Mr President

I want you to know I pray for you
And I care for you personally, too.
People judge, and people condemn
Without looking at the real problem.
I don't really think that people see
How you are trying so hard to set us free.
Free from recession and from debt
From being controlled and kept
None of which you even created
But are trying to get us again liberated.
Don't listen to those that nag and naysay
For they couldn't even stand in your shoes for a day.
Is it his fault there's a recession?
If not, then stop this tirade and procession.
You were the problem starters yourselves!
Who are you to crawl into his life and delve?
Yes, his platform might not be all perfect
But that doesn't make him a reject.
Let him that is without sin cast the first stone;
If not, then leave the man alone!
Hate, malice, and ill will are all that are thrown
To all in power and those with a given crown.
He was placed there by your very own hand;
Now you want to go against and form a band?
Dear Mr. President, I personally pray for you,
And I hope others will start now, too.

# History of the Past

History is repeated over and over again
All of the strife, fear, and unbearable pain.
Can this never-ending, elliptical cycle
Be learned from and this lesson recycled?
To learn our future, we must learn from our past
And finally gain the knowledge needed at last.
Paving out a new road for your future generations
A road of redemption, peace, and regeneration.

# The First Words

A sweet line of words whispered into the air
Every single word having an alternating pair.
So softly said that they were not captured
Yet has had every soul for eternity enraptured.
Forming into existence every single thing
Without practice, care, or even a whim.
Gently, the wind carried the acts spoken away
Saving them for some faraway day.
I myself wonder what those words are
But for now, let the suspense raise the bar.

# The Words We Miss

Sometimes silence is what is eminent;
We just need to take time for the moment.
Putting electronics and gadgets off
And just taking time to think about the days.
Of how we pass through each with nods and okays
Not caring or wondering if something is missing
In those song lyrics that we are always singing.
Lyrics of rare or shallow love with no depth
But those of made-up, imaginary wretches.
Thoughts we wouldn't even consider belted out
And when they come up, we all give a shout.

# A True Home

The road back home, long and weary
The work far more hard and dreary.
The reward coming is precious
The welcome warmth is luscious.
A bright smile awaits
For me, that is home
And when troubles come, I am not alone.
A foot goes before the other in pace;
The destination in sight is the final race.

# Loves Journey

What would you do if someone you loved was dying?
If someone you cared for was heartbreakingly crying
And there was no other solution to this equation
Than to take their pain, suffering, and lamentation?

Could you even attempt this horrendous feat?
It is not even conceivable in the very least
But imagine that a thousand times a thousand.
Shouldn't this act itself be declared contraband?

Love attempted and succeeded at this feat
With love and kindness at the very least;
It took it to the next level above just dying
And without lamentation and even crying.

# Hopes Victory

Hope hears all of our complaints and turns them around;
Hope goes beyond itself and exceeds and abounds.
Discouragement seeks to kill and destroy everything
That Hope had put in every somebody or something.
Within the ashes, Hope arises to bring new life
And ends all of Discouragement's old strife.

# The Future Tomorrow

Shootings have taken the unsuspecting lives of many
Yet now, it's not that weird or uncanny.

Abortions are now publicly and legally sanctioned;
The price of life is being auctioned.

Rape is more abundant and rampant than before
With innocence now like trash on the floor.

War is tearing apart the families of the drafted
This paranormal event skillfully crafted.

"Will these once limited but now frequent acts occur?"
"Yes, there will be a period of peace after the uproar."

# The Master Plan

Actions and reactions are what make or break a man;
Emotions hidden make the best master plan.

The simple smile speaks more than a thousand words;
And one can have but so many precious lords.

Despite the rumors, nations can change in a day
And all it takes is two beings and a way.

So let both shake hands ingenuously and agree
To let themselves go and to live as free.

# The Ugly

It creeps inside of you
Seeking only to subdue
Your inner self-esteem.
It watches and deems
Who is good to please
And who it can tease.
It hates itself though
Hiding in its borough.
Pulling good things down
Is how it keeps its crown.

# The Break of Day

The horrible nightmares and daydreams
And fear-inspiring shadows of the night
Floating in and out like spectral streams.
You're always keeping your head down
Not even looking at the seeds you've sown
Then the sun comes up, bringing its light.
The dreams and shadows are torn apart
Leaving only you, yourself, and your heart.

# A Moment in Time

To enjoy a fleeting moment is almost unheard of;
The ordinary excuse is "There isn't time enough."
The sounds of nature are simply just ignored
And people only care to hear if they are bored.
A second here or there can be a moment shared
With a person to show you love and you care.
Just one moment, still there is no time to spare
And tell me why it always seems be like this
Because you're trying to get things accomplished.
Start putting off the gadgets, devices, and gismos
And sit and take a look at the sparkling cosmos.

# The Strangers

You pass them with signs on the streets
The people that you never think to greet.
The people who serve you in the cafes
Bringing you your caramel mocha lattes.
You treat them like dirty scum and trash
Laughing at them and behaving brash.
One kind word would be greatly advised
Because they could be angels in disguise.

# The Loneliest Person

They're always stuck in a sea of familiar faces
Just counting the time away in slow, timed paces.
People always want an ill-placed piece of them
Will someone finally hear their piercing screams?

One true friend steps up to their trampled hearts
Putting the worn pieces together part by part;
The seed of love begins its long-awaited repair.
All loneliness needed was some tender loving care.

# Titles

Jock, prep, nerd, geek, scene, or emo
Why do we label people we don't even know?

Sir, mister, ma'am, lady, and miss
All seem to be now a vagrant, missed wish.

It seems like instead of showing respect
We only now speak with language that's decrepit.

Instead of focusing on fads and trends
Work on making *our* history better in the end.

# The Leper

Cast out and alone he stands
Beaten, bruised by many hands
Searching for that gentle touch
Wanting to forsake his crutch.

He finds one with kind eyes
Loving, caring, telling no lies
Giving him the life he was due;
Leaving, he looked back at you.

# Opposing Forces

Land and sea
Melody and harmony
You and me
Euphony and cacophony.

All enmities
But in perfect unity
And fluidity
Avoiding their tendencies.

# The Sweet Life

Glamorous, sparkling, and filled with excitement
Or is what the media has been painting it to be?
Their lives are turned into hostile environments
And we begin to see things that we want to see
Disregarding them as true, feeling human beings.

Pointing, laughing, joking at their unveiled lives
Having no idea what a day in their shoes entails
You continue injuring them with bullets and knives
Never caring about the lonely paths that they trail
Dear Mr. Prodigy, wait till the world laughs when you fail.

# Music and Lyrics

Word going though one ear and out of the other;
You think, "If the beat is good, why bother?"
The memory of your brain is underestimated;
The lyrics show if you've watched and waited.
Sing and think about every word you have said
And see if they don't leave you brain-dead.
You can dance, jump, and blare it for everyone
But what about after when that sweet beat is done?

# The Task at Hand

It will be a long night before our work is done;
We can do it together or even all alone.
Two hundred paces to our front, left, and right
With different paths lying side by side.
The task looks even more daunting to us now
But we seem to be detached from it somehow.
It's trying to overtake and stop us in our tracks
Making the wall slam into our backs.
Fighting this great and final foe that we defeat
We turn onto homeward-bound streets.

# The Old Abandoned House

It sits there forlorn and disfigured
Remembering those sweet memories
Of familiar smells that did linger
Bubbling laughter and scary stories
The pitter-patter of innocent feet
Secrets whispered through its doors
The late-night meet and greets
And once despised stained floors.
It awaits for its new companions
Not knowing how undesired it is.

# The True Key

Hurried, you run about
Wishing for a rewind button;
Letting out your shouts
You want time before dawn.
Preparation is truly key
So never let laziness get the lead.

# Making the Difference

One simple word or phrase can change the future
Bringing about the discovery of a life-changing cure;
One simple act of kindness can be life or death
Causing that person to choose his final end or breath.

Shyness, pride, or insecurity is not an excuse at all
When dealing with catching or returning that curveball;
Someone out there desperately does need you
If you don't give up, it might mean they won't want to.

# Works and Deeds

You've bought the materials
Everything needed to make it real.
Imported wood and stone
All to make your spectacular home
Chosen all of the rooms
And every pan, brush, and broom.
Warnings went without heed;
You hadn't even bought its deed.

# Pride

Pride blinds you from seeing what is true;
Pride leads you on paths that are crude
Causing you to lose those close to you.
Pride's path can only be avoided by few;
But even fewer have never trod on it.
For on it lie past king's deaths forfeit
Lures of Pride, stained with others' shame
Try to keep you from Humility's name.

# Unquenchable Thirst

We all have this desire for something more
Something aching in the essence of our core.
Kings and conquerors looked for an answer
As if it were an incurable form of cancer;
There is an unidentified, centralized disease.
Hope—it is the only thing that puts us at ease
And Hope is our only connection to Life.

# The Orphan

She goes from home to home, wanting a warm touch
Feeling emptier every time they reject her in a rush.
Her mother is dead; her father is locked up in jail
And from day to day, her hope seems to wane and pale.
Her heart soon becomes encased in brittle, jagged ice
An innocent who has forgotten the meaning of nice.
You could say it was her own fault and hers to blame
Or you could realize it's her society that is at shame.

# The Ultimate Price

What do you say that the ultimate price is?
Is it wealth, fame, popularity, or nice things?
The true, ultimate price is what you have now
Breath, life, joy, the ability to kneel and bow
So instead of complaining about what is wrong
Enjoy the life you live among the throng.

# The Remnants

They are the ones who never leave your side
Who stay for more than just the free ride.
Those who are the ever-supportive friends
Who never take more than willing to lend.
The few, the proud, the eternally prized
Those that in the end will above others rise.
Those who are in their numbers very rare
And who are willing to stand up despite jeers.

# Knowledge

Easily gained but not readily used
Knowledge is not to be perused;
Pointing the way to Wisdom's path
Knowledge can not be led to wrath.
It is ignored and often cruelly abused
When its ways are used as a subtle ruse.
It is the only key to Wisdom's latch
And therefore the unhidden catch.

# Living Examples

No governments or secret agencies
Yet they live naturally without treaties.
What can then be said for man's ways
When all we do is number our days?
They were put with us for a reason
And let us learn from them in season.

# The Perpetrator

They stand in your halls causing confusion
Chaos and disorder in mass profusion.

Their fake smiles are why they're skilled
And how their reputations are never killed.

Their true faces are hidden under their persona;
Broken, the shards fall off of their corona.

It's harder to hide the true person hidden inside;
Than to let your true spirit show outside.

# The Producer

Every *t* must be crossed and *i* dotted
And no mistakes must be spotted.
He'll give you a break once in a while
But then it's back to the files.
Luckily, you have a get-out-of-jail card;
The curtains close as you end your part.

# Work

The object should be one of happiness
A thing not done out of laziness.
You should do it as if for yourself
With love being able to be felt.
As a gesture of absolute sincerity
Instead of one done forlorn and in pity.

# Five Types of Truth

The Absolute Truth is the one most loved
And the Half Truth second to the above.
An Ounce of Truth, the casual retort
The Chalice of Truth, found in records
And the Twisted Truth which is the worst lie.

# The Loveliest Sounds

Beautiful choirs sing;
Church bells ring.
Bird quietly hum;
Rain beats its drum.
The loveliest sound
Is laughter, loud.

# Automotive Personalities

The old, worn car and his gentle spirit
The flashy convertible going with the drift
The tall, beautiful SUV, the graceful gazelle
The proud luxury car, too profitable to sell.

# Darkness

Not all that is clothed in darkness is sin
But simply means Light cloaking its bright sheen.
For as quickly as it disappeared in your sight
It can come in the blink of an eye just as bright.
Darkness is but a temporary state for now
Yet Light can always seem to dispel it somehow.

# The Leader

The leader was once a follower
A sidekick, and a shadower.
He learned from the best the way
To talk, walk, teach every day.
Noting what to improve or take
And how to notice the snake.
He wasn't brave or courageous
But saw what was dangerous
And smart and made the change.
Following isn't at all strange
But know it cannot stay that way.

# The Almighty Dollar

They say that money makes the world go round
But soon it becomes the chains in which we are bound.
Money also feeds the hungry and clothes the poor
But it causes bodies to hit the crimson floors.
With the good also comes the horrifying bad
But most of it seems lost on trends and fads.

# Prosperity

Many seek this life-altering word
Not knowing they're hanging from a thin cord.
Responsibility is a must to obtain
So you won't take a detour to Poverty Lane.
Prosperity, O Prosperity
If only people knew to use you without temerity.

# The Double Rainbow

The double promise symbol
As binding as thread and needle
Smiles spread as eyes catch
A single colorfully placed patch.
In the gloom of all the rain
It appears to ease away the pain.

# The Reaper

He comes when all is silent and quiet
To take what are his in dark of nigh;

He waits till the bells of the second tip
To avoid sobbing pleas and angry quips.

No records about him are in our history
Remaining to this world a hazy mystery.

Forever, he waits in the background
Waiting for the end to come around.

# Teachers

Beings that mold the future of our society
Whom we only gift with anger and hypocrisy;
People who were filled with burning fire
Have had their souls torn and filled with ire.

So for the whole world, I say thank you
For those bickering parents, I say thank you
For your past students, I say thank you
This is a shining medal for you brave and few.

# Our Country Tis of Thee

'Tis of thee that there was a war for freedom of speech
'Tis of thee that we fought to openly think and to teach.
'Tis of thee that we wanted to have freedom of religion.
'Tis of thee that safeguarded moving from any region.
'Tis of thee that many are seeking to elect their officials.
'Tis of thee that many were ready to fight for your trials.

# Rain

Rain washes the stains and the pain away;
It gives life to the dawn of another day,
Heals the many scars of Earth's heart,
And then stops and waits quietly for its part.

# Authors Biography

Royal Chukwudumebi is a fourteen-year-old tenth grader who loves to reflect and to write. She developed a passion for writing poetry and fiction at the age of nine and, having identified the techniques of the genre, started developing her own style. She is the author of over a hundred poems, and she also loves to write fiction—even with a touch of spirituality for people. Royal has remarked that her poems are often predicated by "real-life events." She writes with an apparent effortless fluidity of both fashion and technique. Her work repeatedly shifts focus from the beauty and splendor of life to life's demises and failures. On one hand, Royal's work has been compared to that of adults by several critics for her strong emotional stance, which she skillfully subsumes rather than overtly preaches in her work. On the other, she has been praised by other critics for "writing with much understanding." Royal herself, though acknowledging both viewpoints, says she would rather call herself "a teenager."

Royal won first place in Virginia State in the American Association of Christian Schools' National Essay and Poetry Contest (May 3, 2010), Class Top English Student Award (2010), Class Top Speller Award (Language Art Achievement Certificate 2010), citizenship award in recognition of exemplary behavior and valuable services (2008, 2009, 2010), Freshman Class Top Algebra 1 Student (2010), and the Honor Roll Award (2006, 2007, 2008, 2010). It is also noteworthy to add that, in 2009, Royal received the Outstanding Academic Excellence Award and a letter signed by President Barrack Obama.

Royal's passion for books is known to all, and she currently resides in Richmond, Virginia, with her mother.